W9-AGY-726

50+

Math Puzzles & Logic Problems

… A Special Equation Math Puzzles For Kids Ages 8-10 (A Math Puzzles And Brainteasers Grades 6-8) And Math Puzzles For Teens!

By
Jay Johnson

COPYRIGHT NOTICE

Copyright ©2018 by Jay Johnson

All rights reserved. No portion of this book may be reproduced- Mechanically, electronically or by any other means, including photocopying- without written permission of the publisher.

Cover by Eljays Design Concept

Printed in the United States of America

First printing April 2018

TABLE OF CONTENTS

INTRODUCTION 2

PUZZLES 7

SOLUTIONS 56

BACK END BOOK PROMOTION 66

Introduction

Here in these new 50+Math Puzzles & Logic Problems ... A Special Equation Math Puzzles for Kids Ages 8-10 (A Math Puzzles and Brainteasers Grades 6-8) And Math Puzzles for Teens! ...you have access to a special collection of Math Puzzles and Brainteasers put together for kids' math activities.

Without doubt, this is a collection of easy math puzzles that is packaged to challenge kids mind and increase their reasoning capacity!

And before I forget, please note that the answers for all puzzles can be found at the back of the book. This book is recommended for kids ages 8 and up who like a bit of logic challenges... just, as in the case of adults who like some math challenge to while away time!

That is it...now, go ahead, and get a copy for your kids... start solving the puzzles. Have fun. Enjoy!

INSTRUCTION

Try to fill in the missing numbers. You can *use only the numbers from 1 through 4 to complete the equations*. Besides, note that each number is only used once!
Moreover, beware that each row is a math equation; **to solve the equations you will need to work from left to right** And each column is also a math equation; **to solve the equations you will need to work from top to bottom.**

- *Remember that multiplication and division are performed before addition and subtraction.*

Example

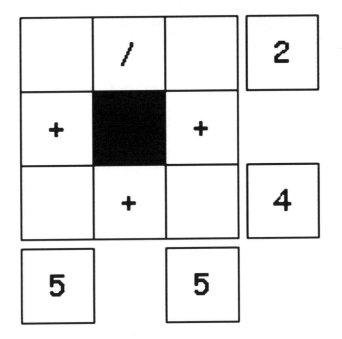

Solution

4	/	2	2
+	■	+	
1	+	3	4
5		5	

Clue!

To start solving the puzzles in this collection, you will need to disregard the **BODMAS rule**! Yes, just for this puzzles… this is a kind of logic teaser. However, you need to take one equation at a time, either vertically or horizontally. That is, solve the equation by the Columns or by the Rows.

But, remember from the instructions above you can only solve the rows equations from left to right and solve the columns equations from top to bottom.

Therefore from the example above, solving by the rows, I can start with row 1:

$4 / 2 = 2$

Now, solving the second Row:

We have $1 + 3 = 4$

If you got the puzzle right the equations will balance out whether you solve them by columns or by rows.

PUZZLE 1

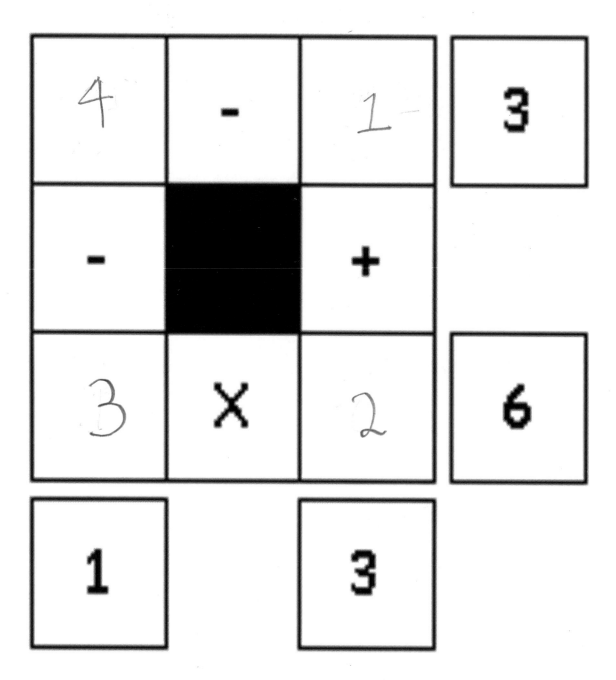

PUZZLE 2

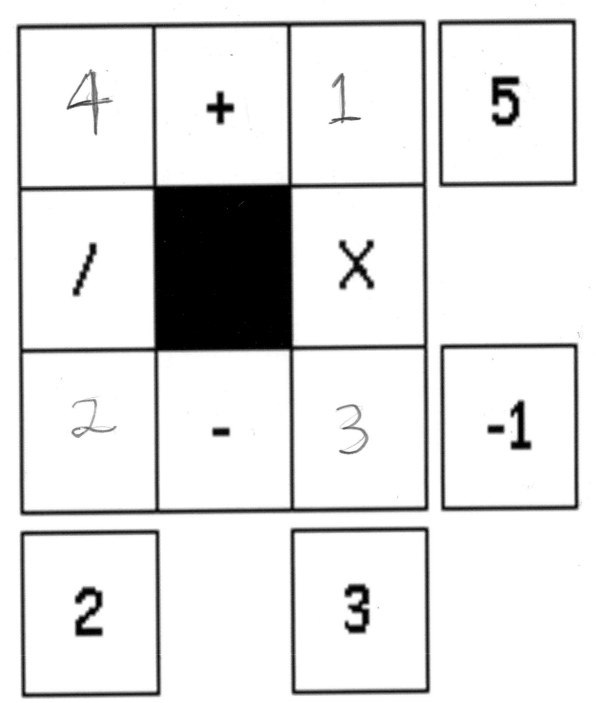

PUZZLE 3

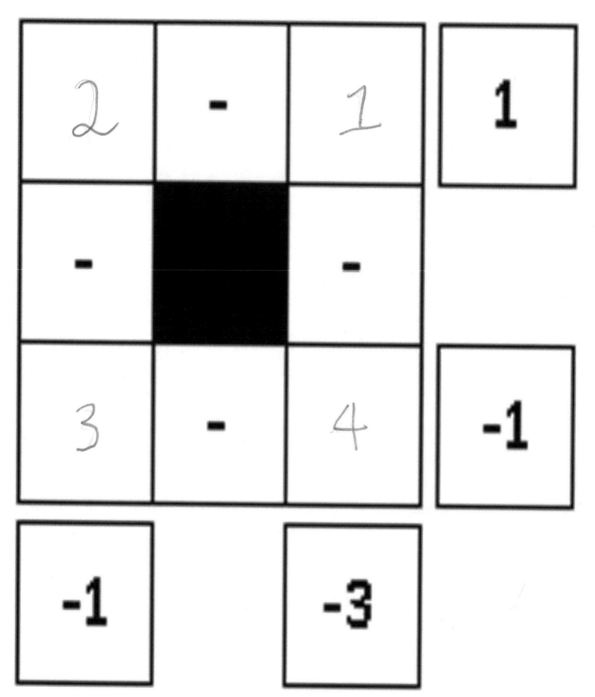

2	-	1	**1**
-		-	
3	-	4	**-1**
-1		**-3**	

PUZZLE 4

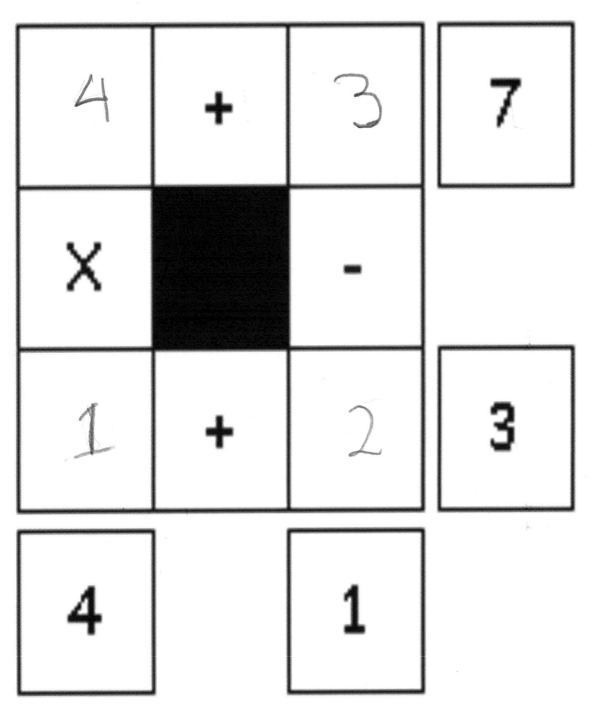

PUZZLE 5

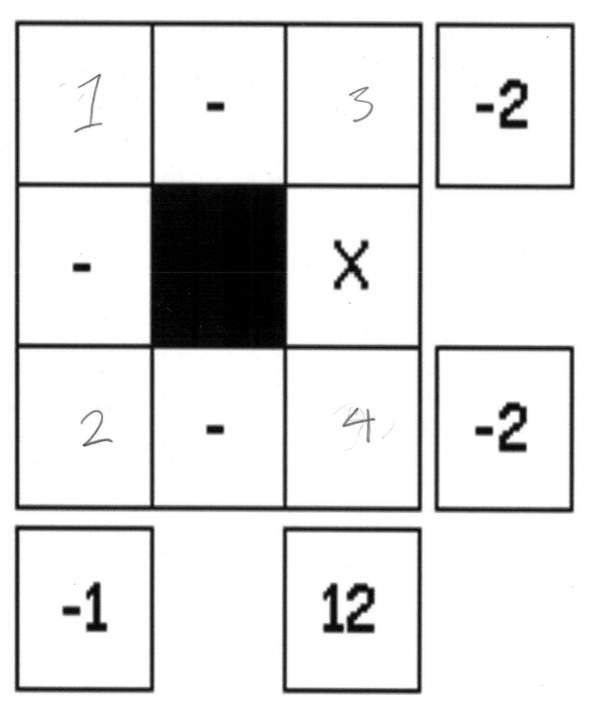

PUZZLE 6

PUZZLE 7

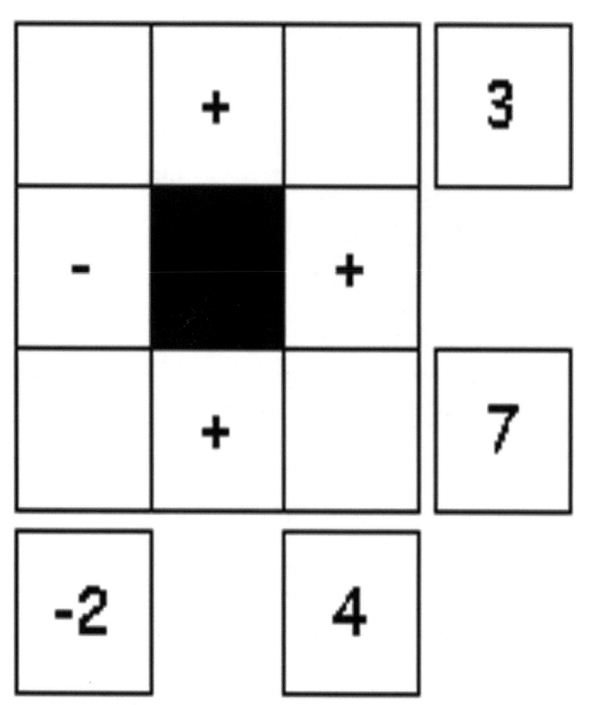

PUZZLE 8

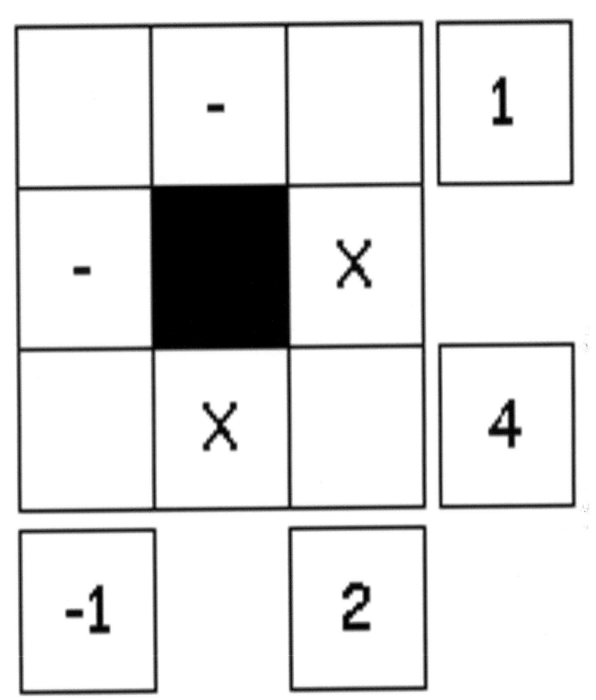

PUZZLE 9

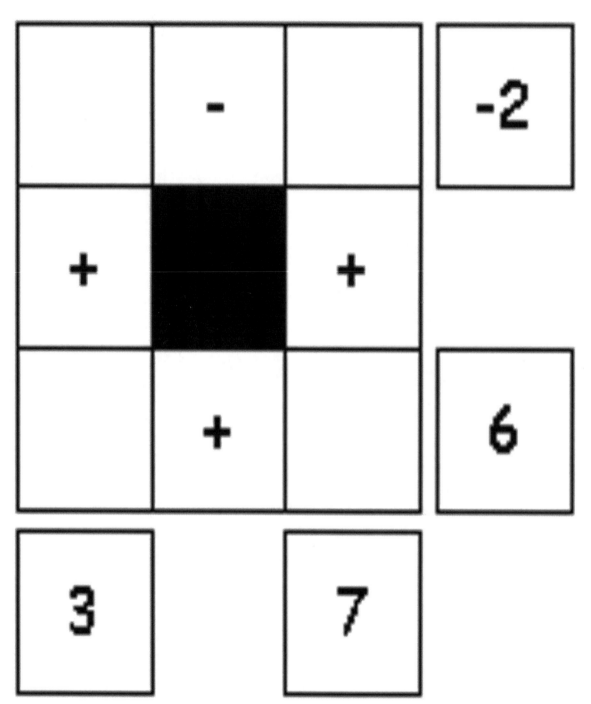

PUZZLE 10

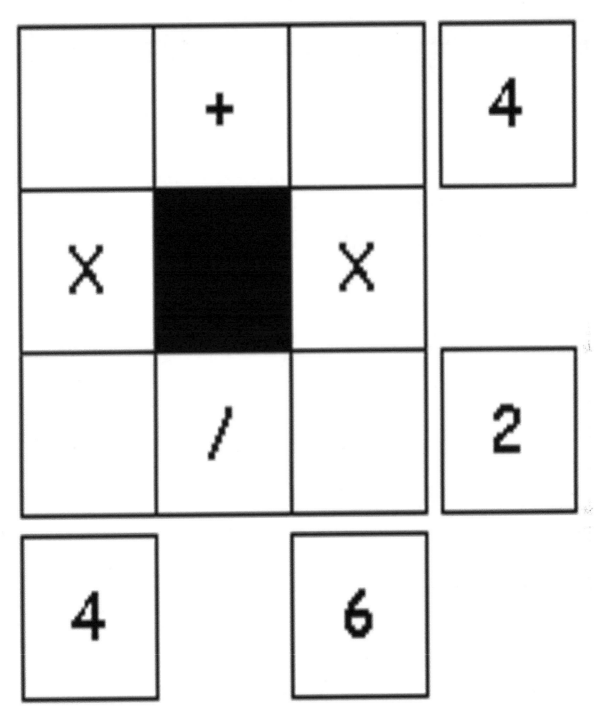

PUZZLE 11

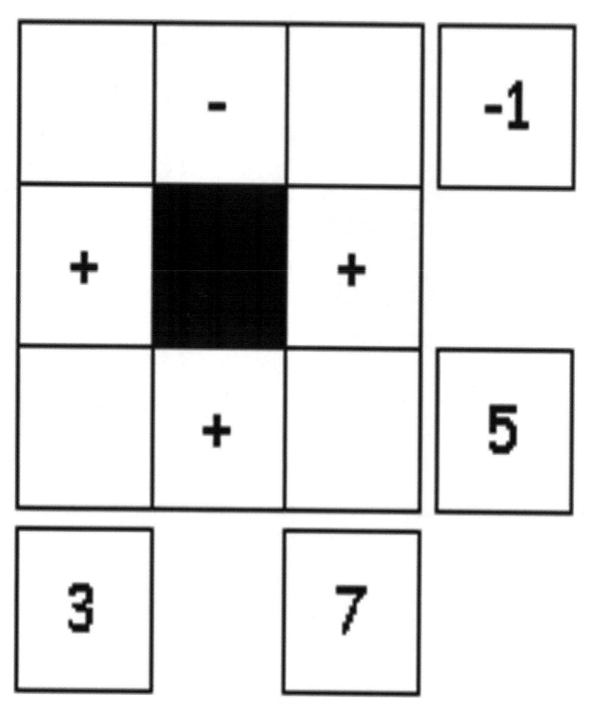

PUZZLE 12

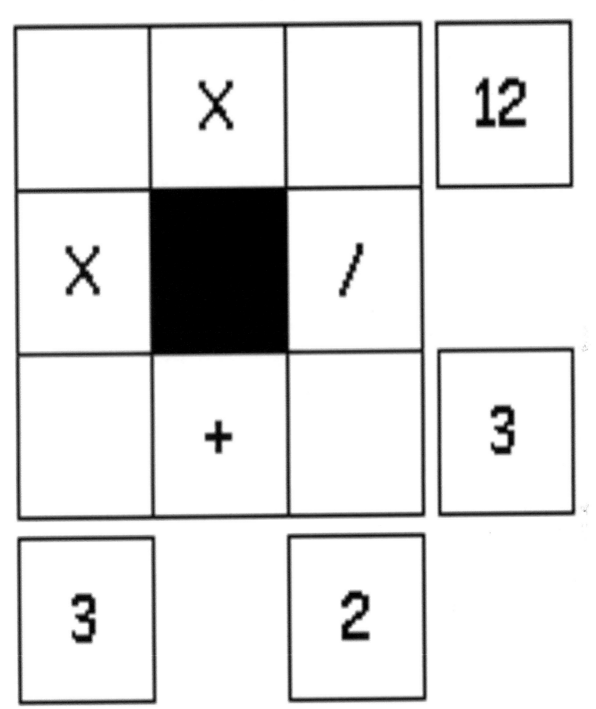

PUZZLE 13

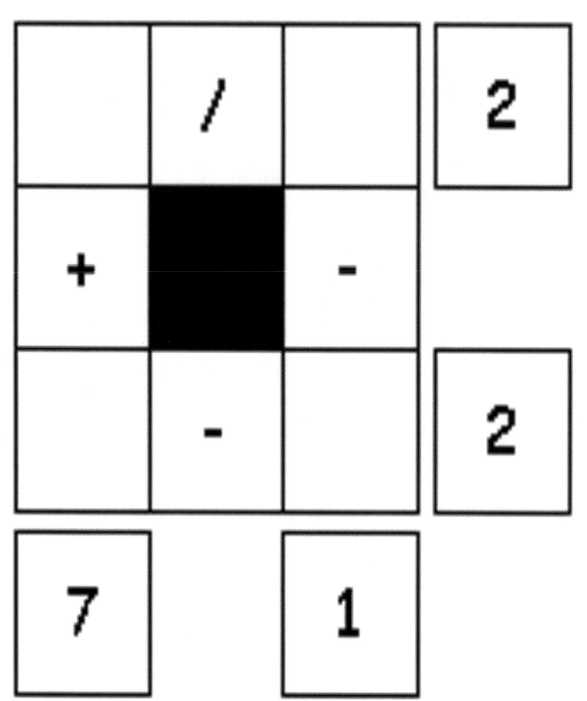

PUZZLE 14

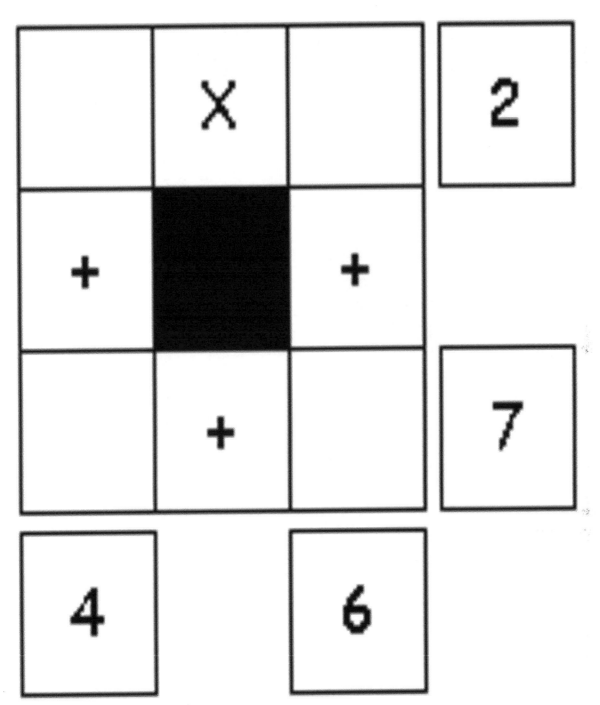

PUZZLE 15

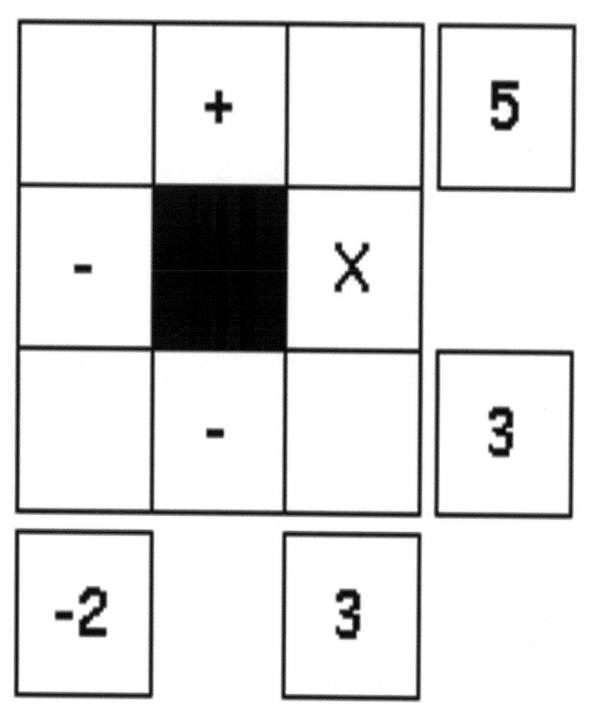

PUZZLE 16

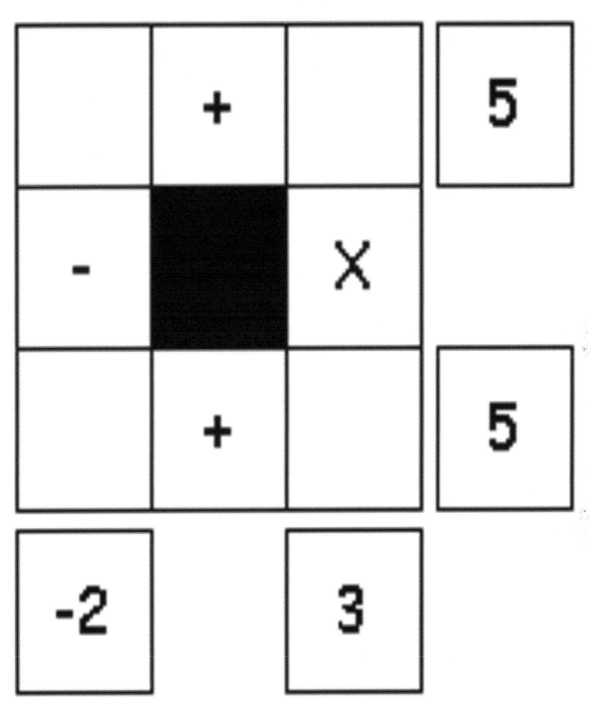

PUZZLE 17

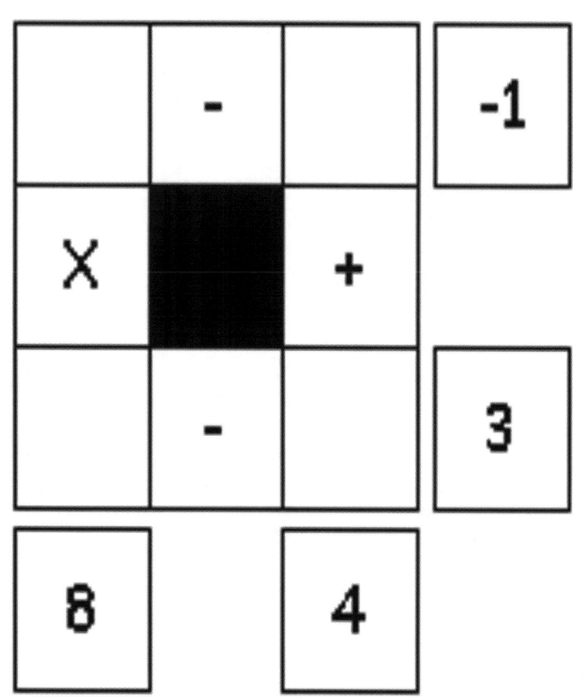

PUZZLE 18

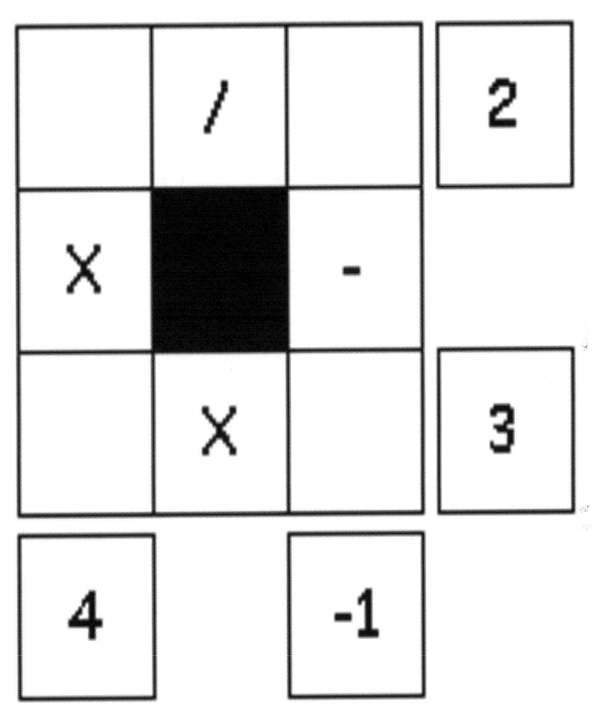

PUZZLE 19

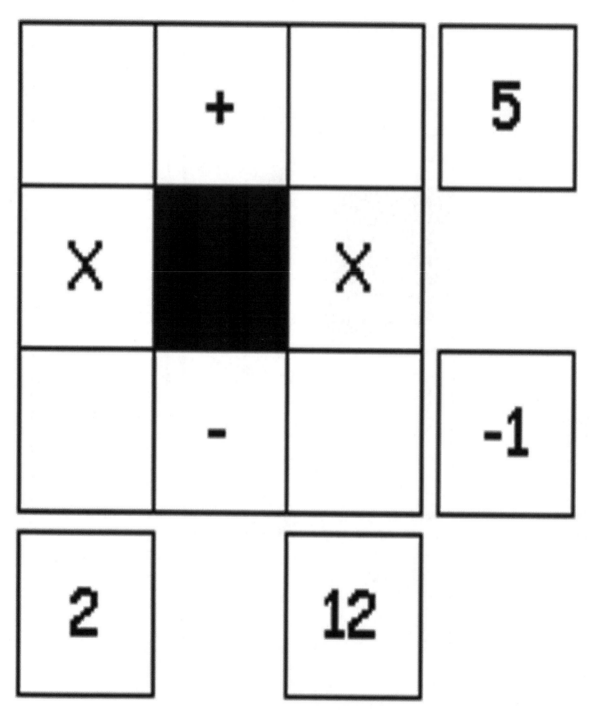

PUZZLE 20

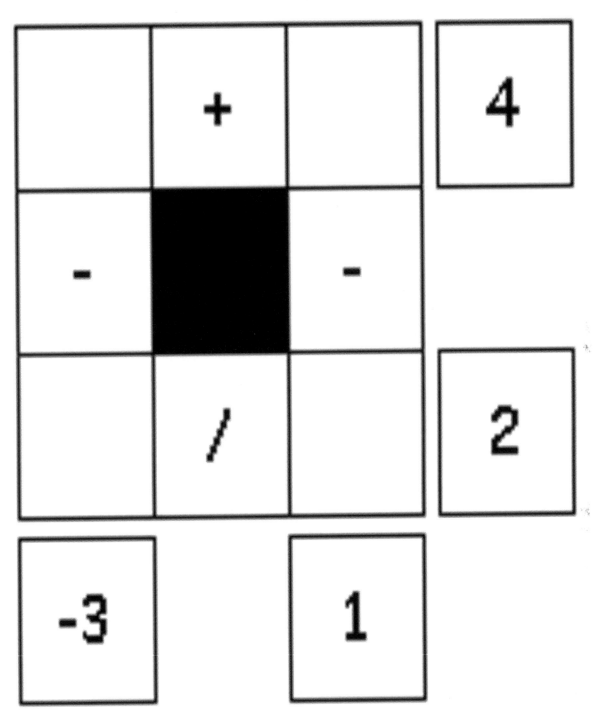

PUZZLE 21

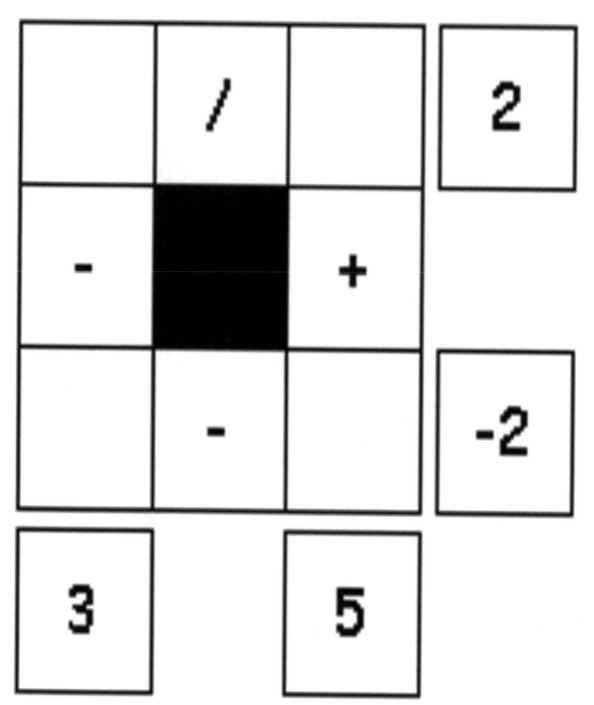

PUZZLE 22

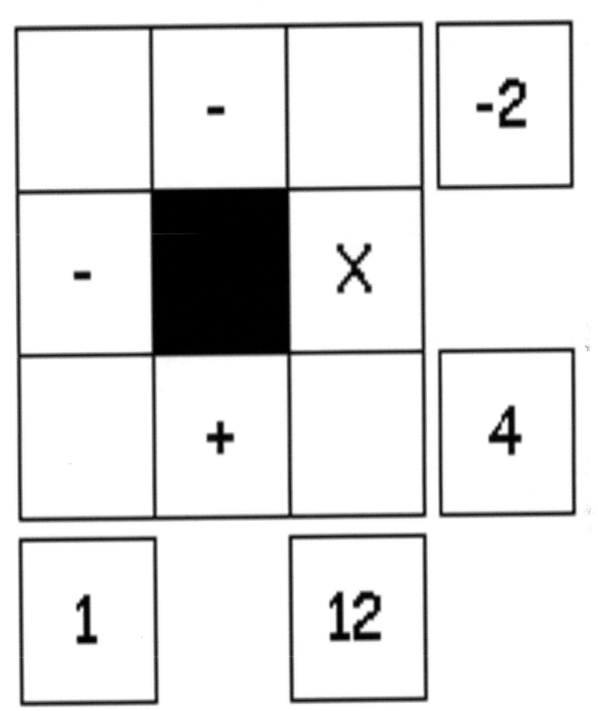

PUZZLE 23

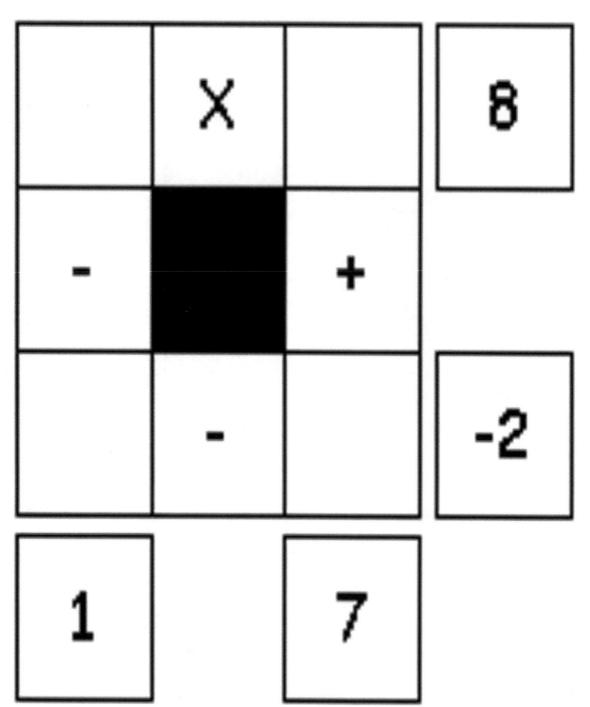

PUZZLE 24

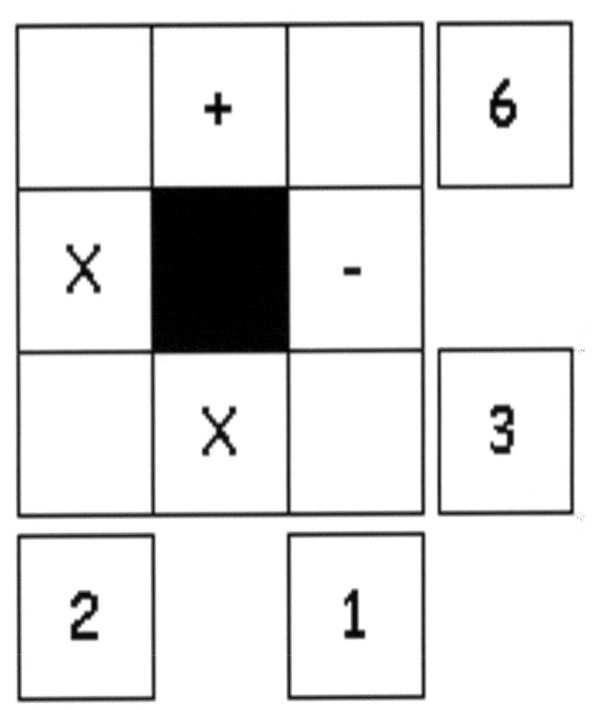

PUZZLE 25

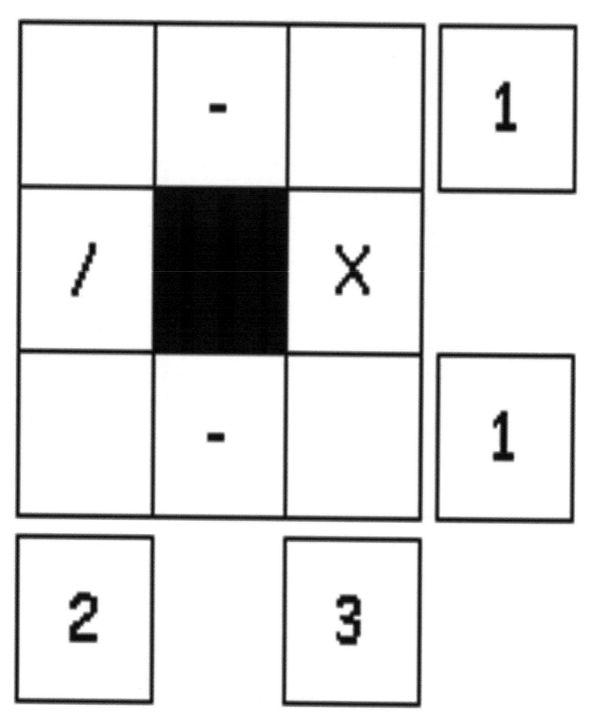

PUZZLE 26

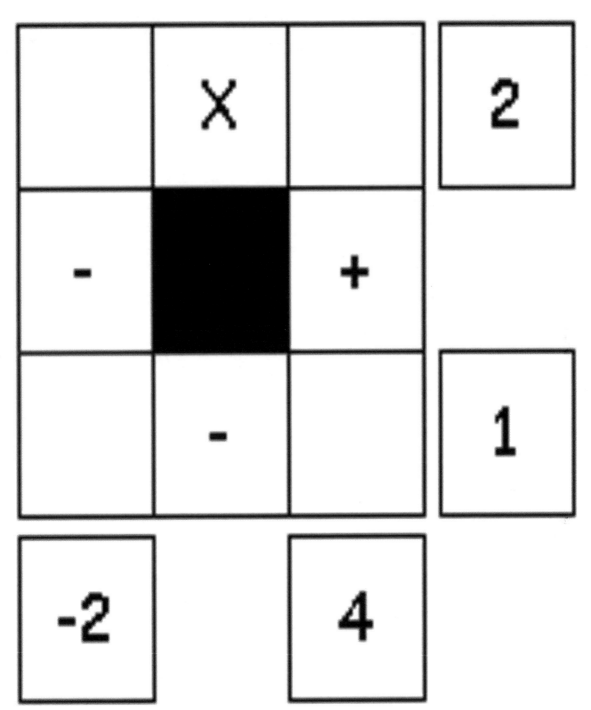

PUZZLE 27

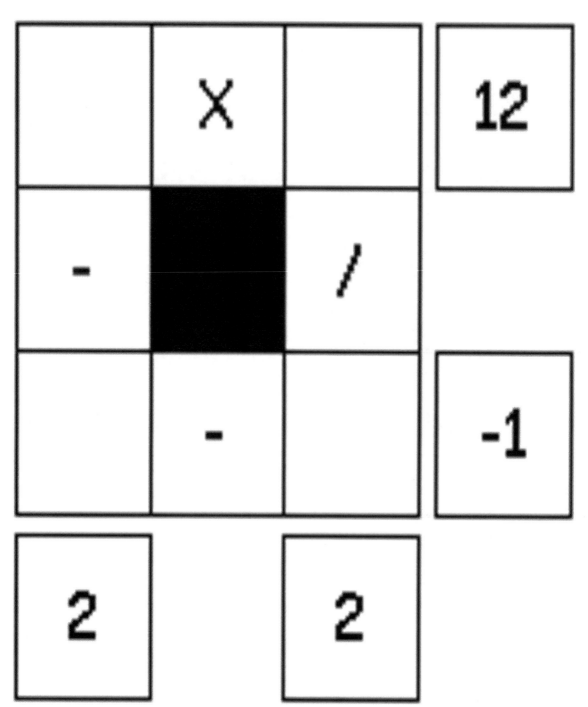

PUZZLE 28

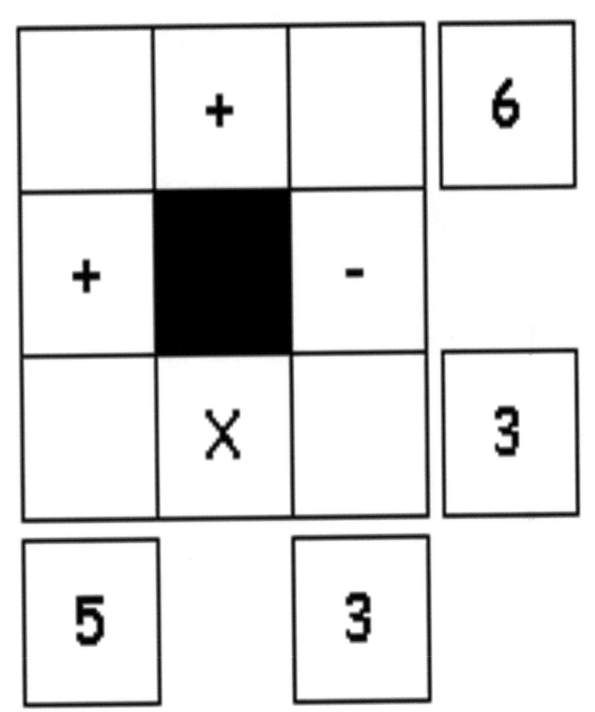

PUZZLE 29

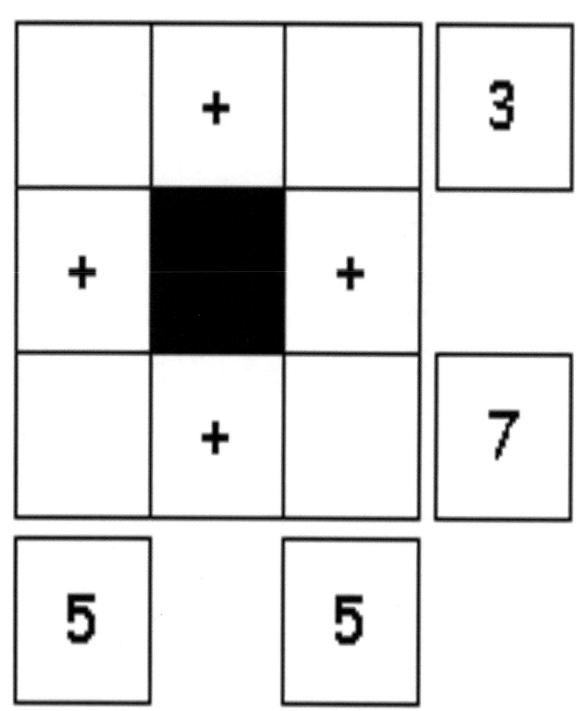

PUZZLE 30

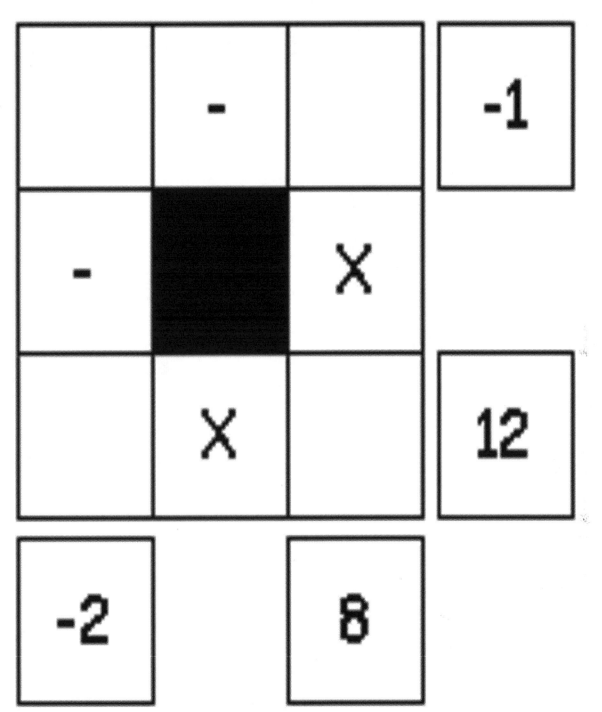

PUZZLE 31

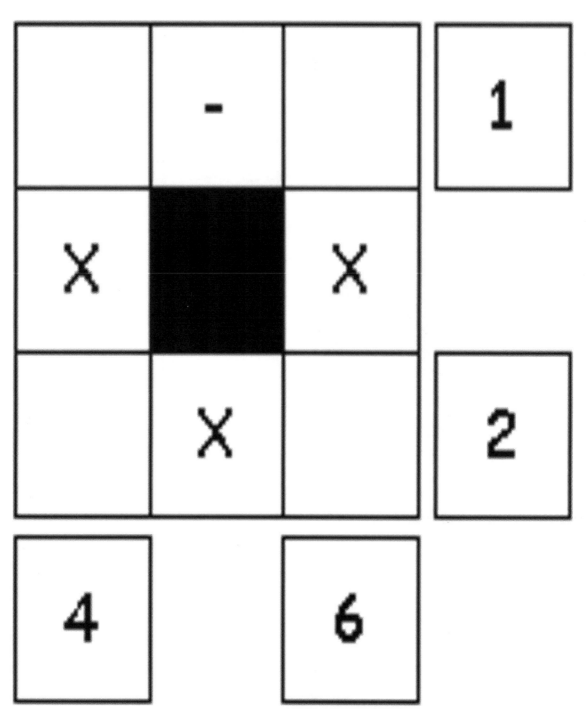

PUZZLE 32

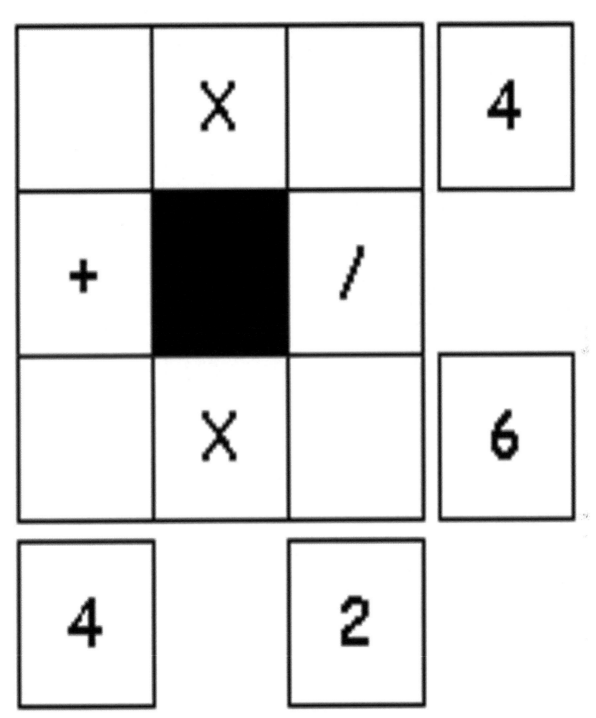

PUZZLE 33

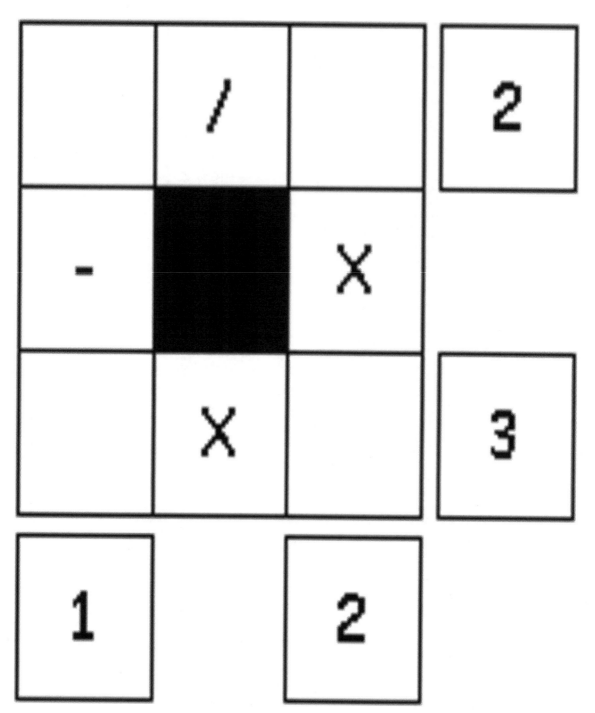

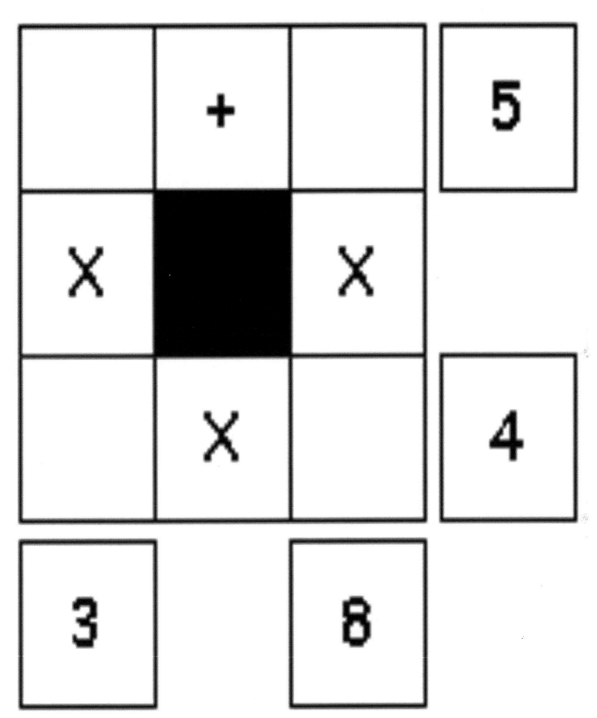

PUZZLE 35

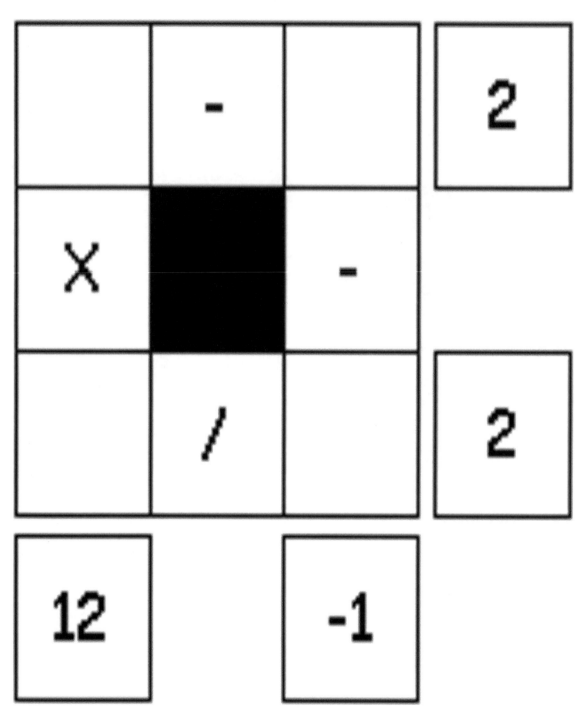

PUZZLE 36

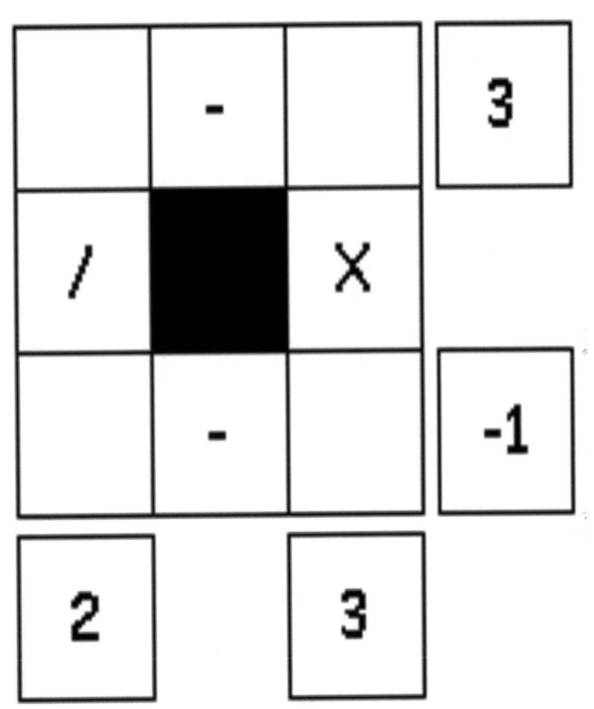

PUZZLE 37

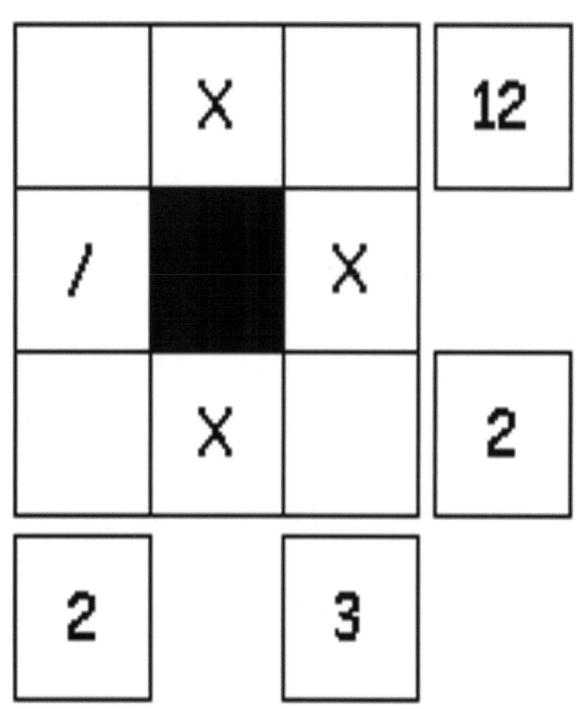

PUZZLE 38

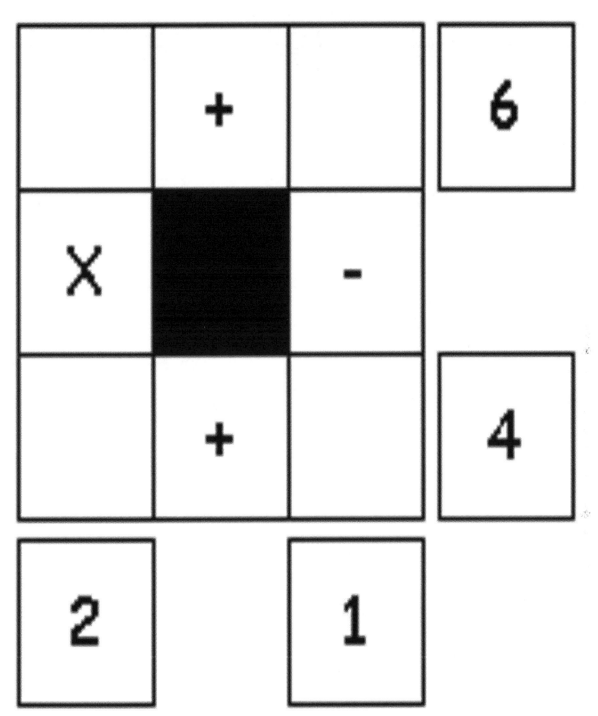

PUZZLE 39

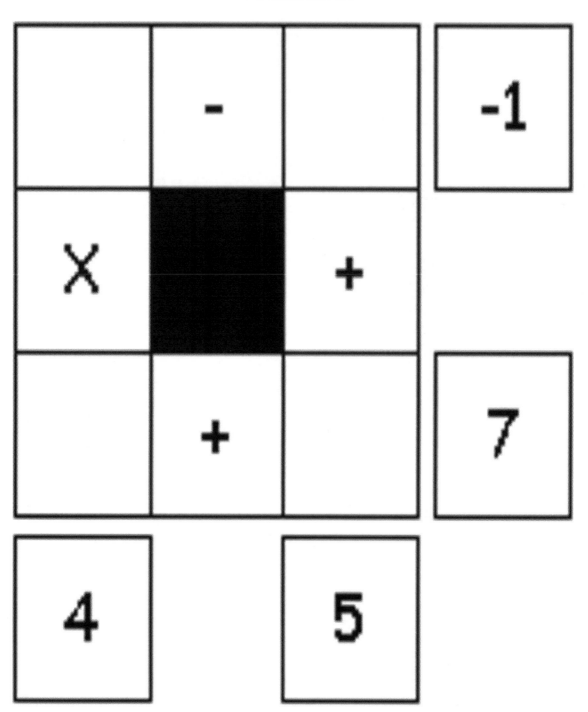

PUZZLE 40

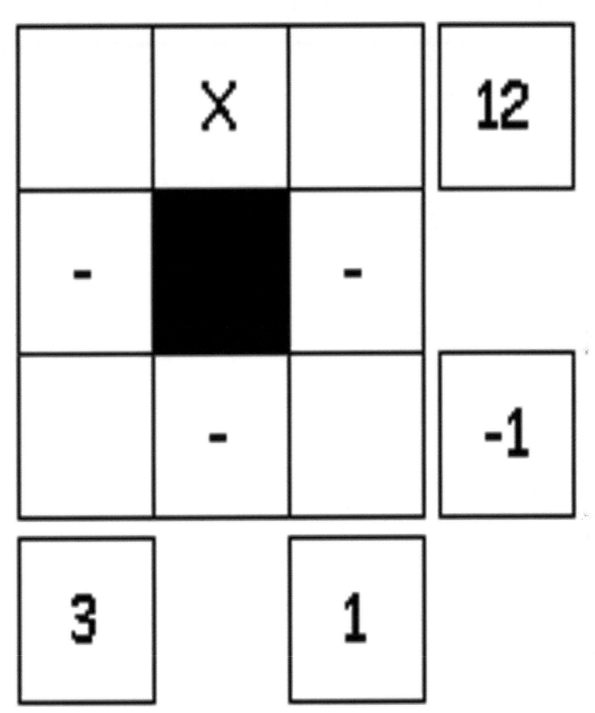

PUZZLE 41

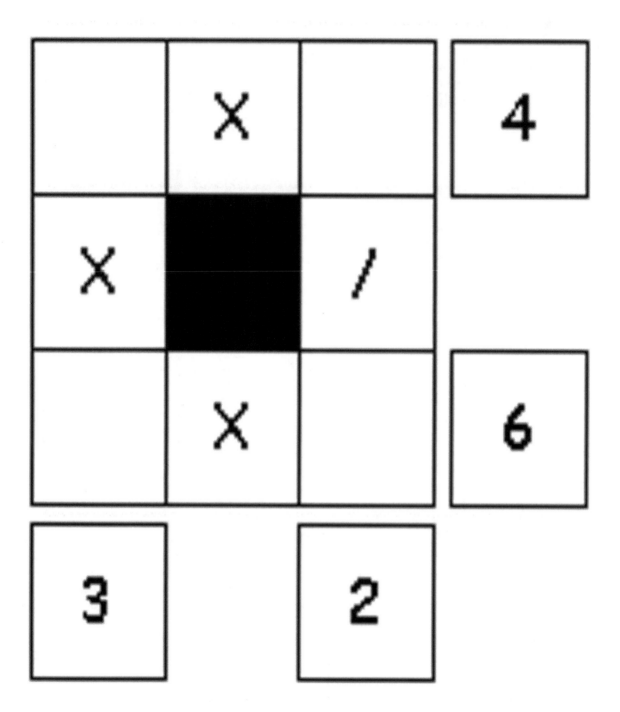

PUZZLE 42

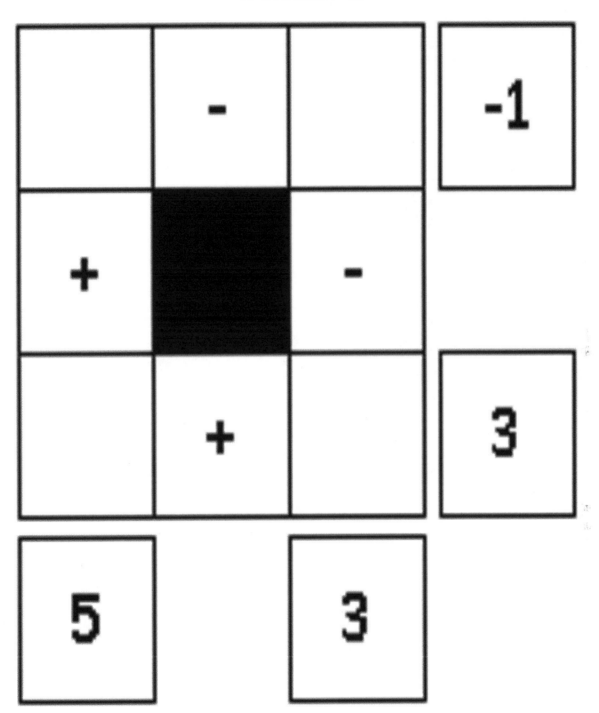

PUZZLE 43

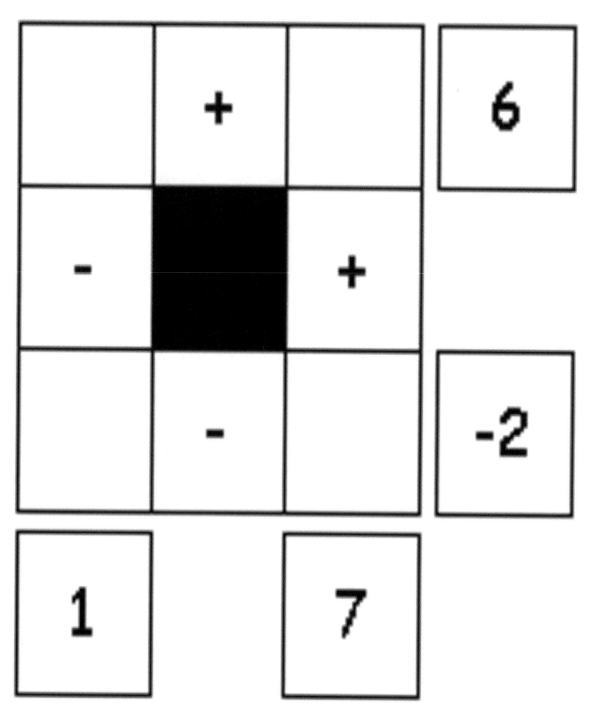

PUZZLE 44

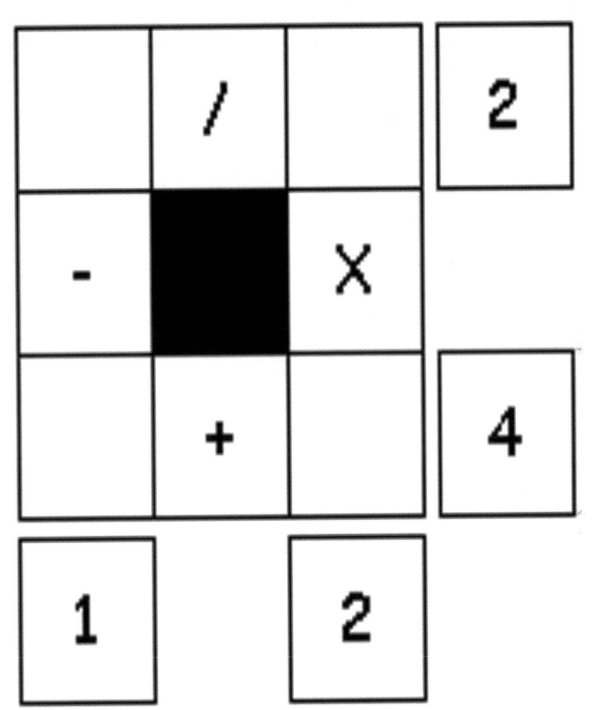

PUZZLE 45

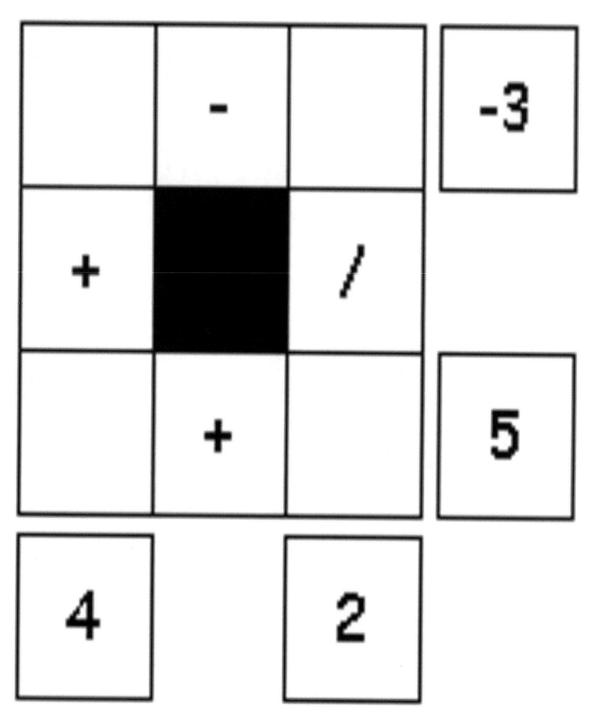

PUZZLE 46

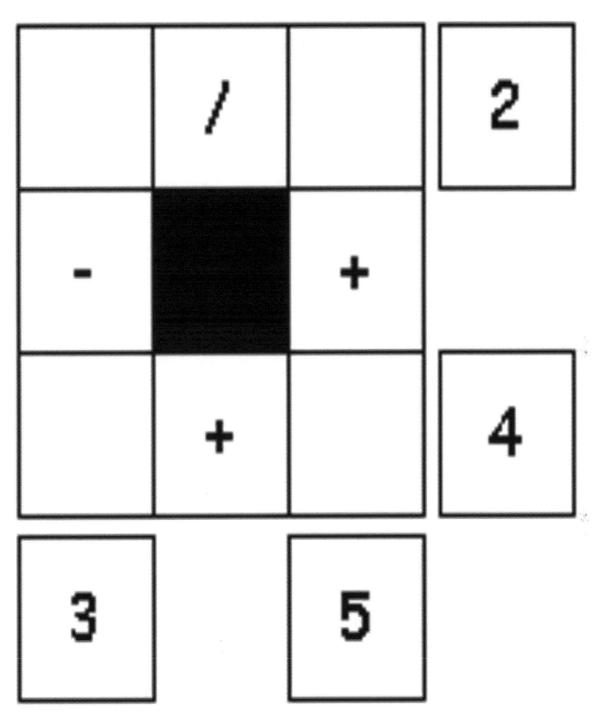

PUZZLE 47

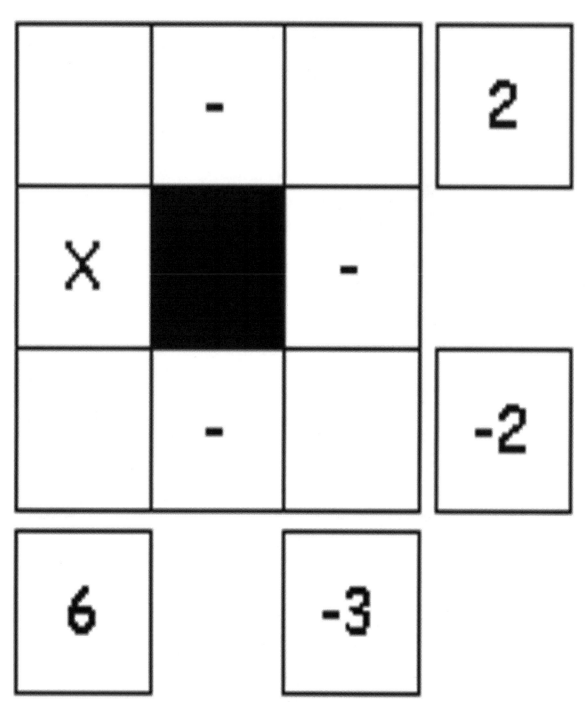

PUZZLE 48

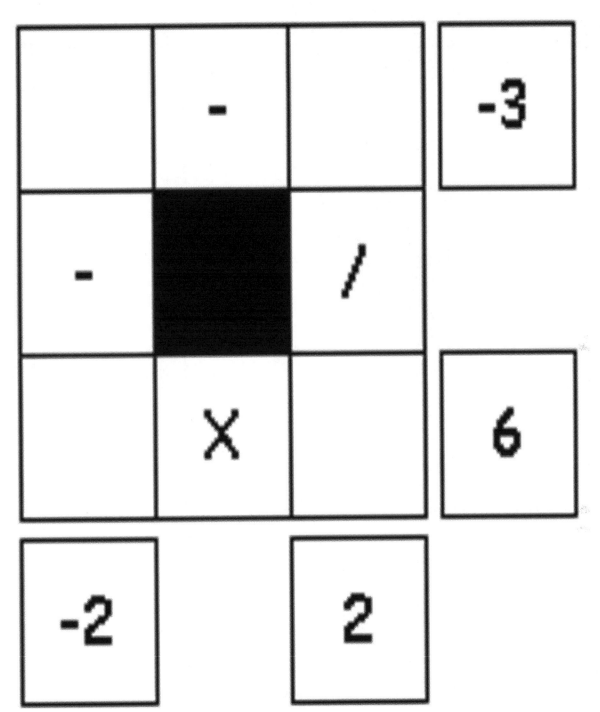

PUZZLE 49

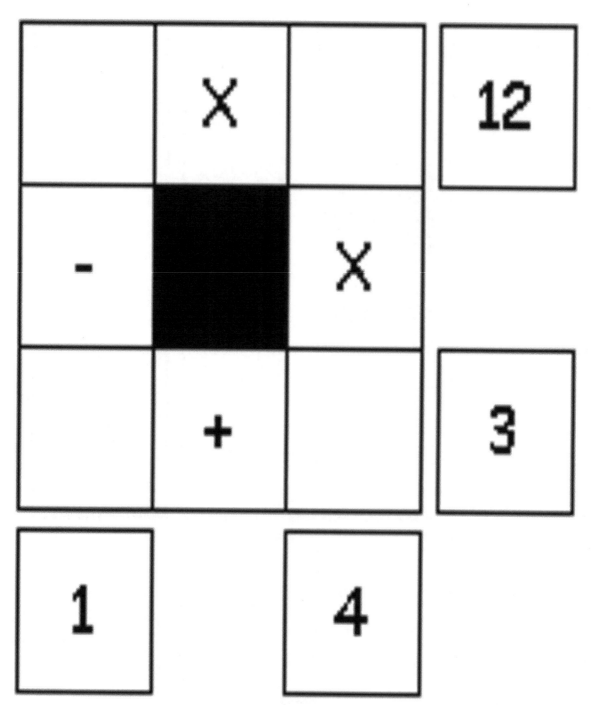

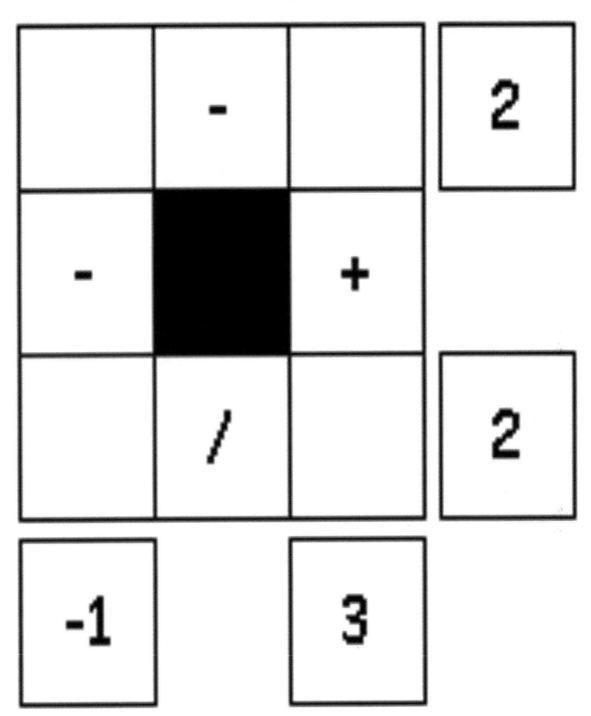

PUZZLE 51

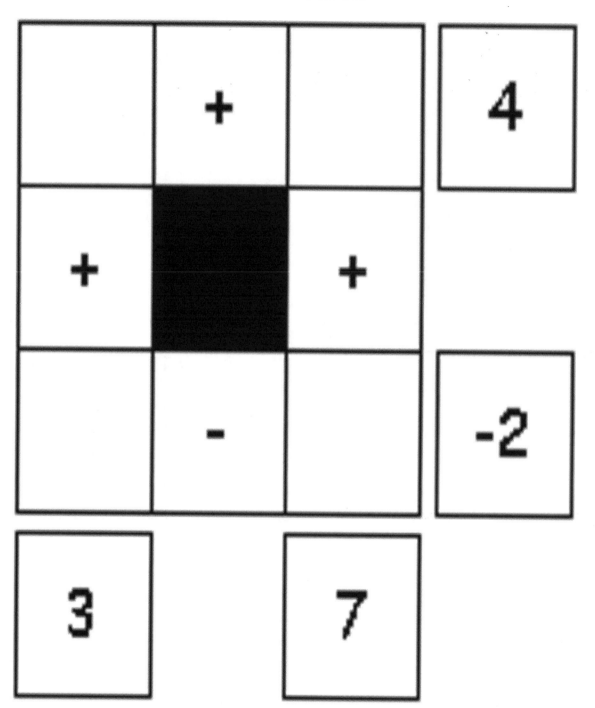

PUZZLE 52

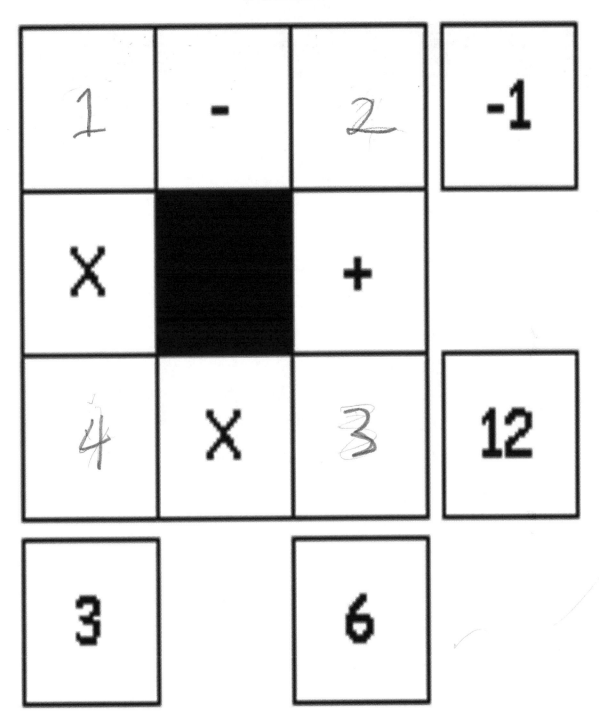

SOLUTIONS

To

The

PUZZLES

PUZZLE 1

4	−	1	**3**
−	■	+	
3	×	2	**6**
1		**3**	

PUZZLE 2

	−		**-2**
−	■	×	
	−		**-2**
-1		**12**	

PUZZLE 3

2	−	1	**1**
−	■	−	
3	−	4	**-1**
-1		**-3**	

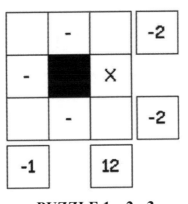

PUZZLE 1 – 2 - 3

PUZZLE 4

4	+	3	**7**
×	■	−	
1	+	2	**3**
4		**1**	

PUZZLE 5

1	−	3	**-2**
−	■	×	
2	−	4	**-2**
-1		**12**	

PUZZLE 6

4	×	3	**12**
×	■	−	
1	×	2	**2**
4		**1**	

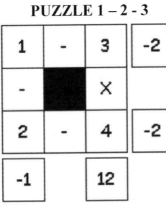
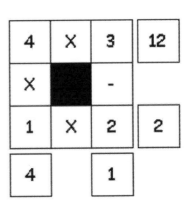

PUZZLE 4 – 5 - 6

PUZZLE 7

2	+	1	**3**
−	■	+	
4	+	3	**7**
-2		**4**	

PUZZLE 8

3	−	2	**1**
−	■	×	
4	×	1	**4**
-1		**2**	

PUZZLE 9

1	−	3	**-2**
+	■	+	
2	+	4	**6**
3		**7**	

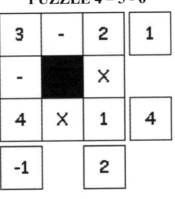

PUZZLE 7 – 8 – 9

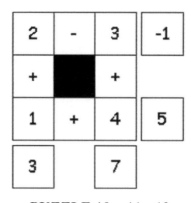

PUZZLE 10 – 11 - 12

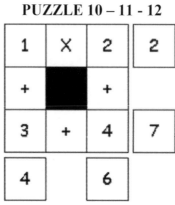

PUZZLE 13 – 14 - 15

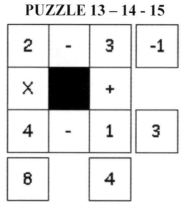

PUZZLE 16 – 17 – 18

60

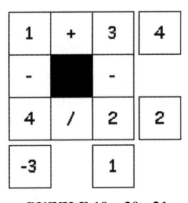
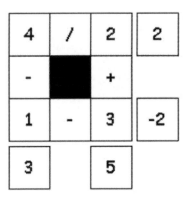

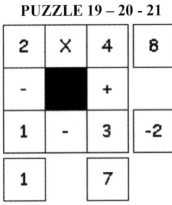
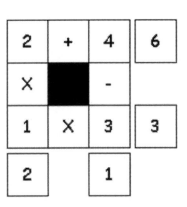

PUZZLE 19 – 20 - 21

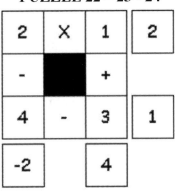

PUZZLE 22 – 23 - 24

PUZZLE 25 – 26 – 27

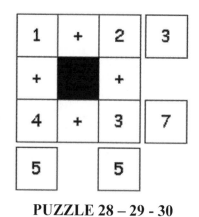

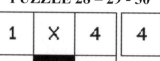

PUZZLE 28 – 29 - 30

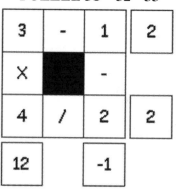

PUZZLE 31 – 32 - 33

3	+	2	5
X		X	
1	X	4	4
3		8	

3	-	1	2
X		-	
4	/	2	2
12		-1	

4	-	1	3
/		X	
2	-	3	-1
2		3	

PUZZLE 34 – 35 – 36

62

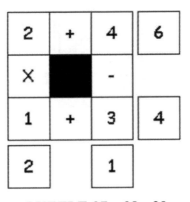

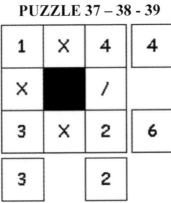

PUZZLE 37 – 38 - 39

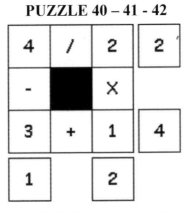

PUZZLE 40 – 41 - 42

PUZZLE 43 – 44 – 45

63

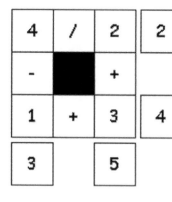 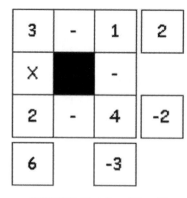

PUZZLE 46 – 47 - 48

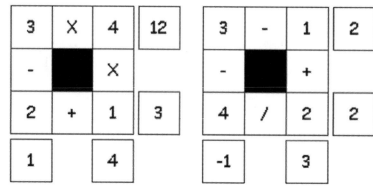

PUZZLE 49 – 50

PUZZLE 51 – 52

64

Thanks for your patronage…Check this other book by same Author on Amazon.com

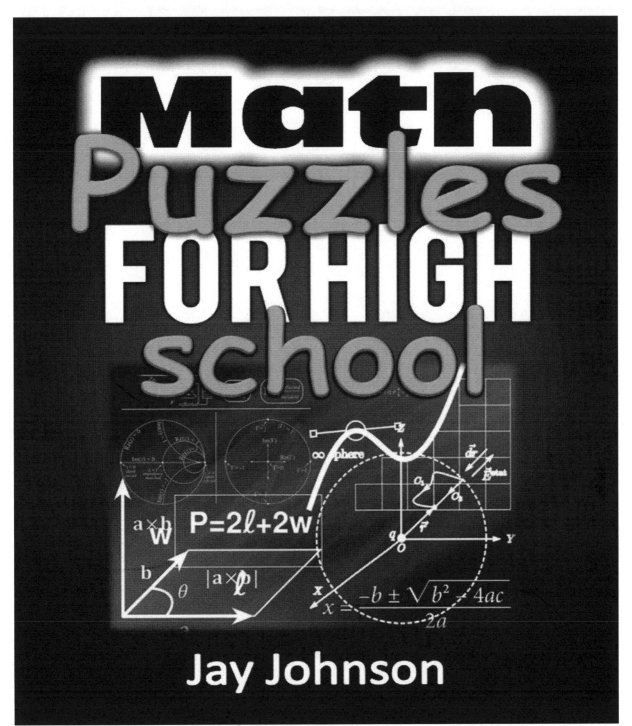

Made in the USA
Middletown, DE
24 August 2020

16406919R00042